ALL ABOUT KU-649-247

THE
SPANISH ARMADA
1588

PAM ROBSON

MACDONALD YOUNG BOOKS

TIMELINE

1558 *Elizabeth I becomes Queen of England*

1577-80 *Francis Drake sails around the world*

1582 *Gregorian calendar is adopted by most of Europe*

1584 *Waghenaer's first sea atlas is published*

1587

    February *Execution of Mary Queen of Scots*

    April *Drake attacks Spanish ships in Cadiz harbour*

1588

    May *Spanish Armada sets sail from Lisbon*

    22 July *English fleet anchors in Plymouth Sound*

    29 July *Spanish Armada sights Lizard Point*

    30 July *Armada is sighted in Plymouth Sound*

    31 July *Action off Plymouth*

    1-2 August *Action off Portland Bill*

    3-4 August *Action off the Isle of Wight*

    7 August *Spanish anchor off Calais*
          English send fireships into Calais harbour

    8 August *Battle of Gravelines*

    19 August *Elizabeth I addresses her troops at Tilbury*

    21 August *Driven north by storms, Spanish ships sail
          for Spain*

    26 October *The last ship of the Armada, the* Girona,
          sinks off the Irish coast

1603 *Death of Queen Elizabeth I*

1752 *England adopts the Gregorian calendar*

1944 *The D-Day 'armada' reaches the Normandy beaches*

All dates follow the New Style (NS) Gregorian calendar

ALL ABOUT...

THE
SPANISH ARMADA
1588

PAM ROBSON

Text © Pam Robson 1996

Illustrations © James Field (Simon Girling Associates) 1996

Photographs © Sources credited

© Macdonald Young Books an imprint of Wayland Publishers Limited 1996

First published in Great Britain in 1996 by Macdonald Young Books,
61 Western Road, Hove, East Sussex, BN3 1JD

A CIP catalogue for this book is available from the British Library.

ISBN 0 7500 1830 5 (hbk) 0 7500 2148 9 (pbk)

Editor: Annie Scothern

Designer: Jane Hannath

Picture credits: Wayland - *cover, 10, 18b, 33b, 34t*. Mary Evans Picture Library - *title page, 11b, 12t, 15t, 22b, 23, 25, 30*. The British Library - *6, 12b, 38*. The Bridgeman Art Library - *7, 8t, 16, 19, 22t, 24, 27l, 33t, 34b, 35, 37t, 39, 45b*. The British Museum - *8b*. Michael Holford - *11t, 44*. National Maritime Museum - *13, 26, 32t, 37b*. The National Trust - *14*. Rex Features - *15b*. The Times Newspapers Limited 1994, 'Slave trade returns to haunt architect of Armada victory' - *17b*. Daily Mail, 'Netted, suspects from the armada of greed', Wednesday 21 April 1995 © John Frost - *9b*. The Northern Echo, 'At sea with the invasion armada' (photo courtesy of John Connor, veteran of the Russian convoys, Battle of the Atlantic) - *7b*. Science & Society Picture Library - *18t*. National Portrait Gallery - *27r*. Tony Stone - *41*. Mary Rose Trust - *21*. Ulster Museum - *timeline, contents, 42, 43*. The British Museum - *8b*. Loaned privately from a Lincolnshire church - *45t*.

The author and publishers thank the above for permission to reproduce their photographs.

Printed and bound in Belgium by Proost International Book Production.

Other titles in the *ALL ABOUT...* series:

CONTENTS

FLEETS OF SHIPS

The massive galleons of the Spanish Armada must have presented an awesome sight in the summer of 1588 as they came up the English Channel in a seven-mile-wide crescent shape. The word 'armada' means a fleet of ships. The Spanish Armada was also known at the time as 'The Grand Fleet' and 'The Most Fortunate Fleet'. But this was not to be the case – the Spanish Armada was to be most unfortunate. 'Armada' has now come to signify a powerful naval force, a fleet to be feared.

There may seem to be confusion over the date the Spanish Armada reached England because in 1582 most of mainland Europe changed from the 'Old Style' Julian calendar to the 'New Style' Gregorian one. Britain kept the 'OS' calendar until 1752. The confusion can be seen on this news-sheet. It was printed on 23 July 1588, three days after the Armada was first sighted. Most history books give the date of the sighting as 29 July.

[1]

THE

English Mercurie. Nº 50.

Publiſhed by AUTHORITIE,

For the Prevention of falſe Reportes.

Whitehall, July 23*d* 1588.

EARLIE this Morninge arrived a Meſſenger at Sir *Francis Walſingham's* Office, with Letters of the 22d from the Lorde High Admirall on board the *Ark-Royal,* containinge the followinge materiall Advices.

On the 20th of this Inſtant Capt. *Fleming,* who had beene ordered to cruize in the Chops of the Channell, for Diſcoverie, brought Advice into *Plymouth,* that he had deſcried the *Spaniſh Armada* neare the *Lizard,* makinge for the Entrance of the Channell with a favourable Gale. Though this Intelligence was not received till near foure in the Afternoone, and the Winde at that time blew hard into the *Sound,* yet by the indefatigable Care and Diligence of the Lorde High Admiral, the *Ark-Royal,* with five of the largeſt Frigates, anchored out of the Harbour that very Eveninge. The next Morninge, the greateſt Part of her Majeſtie's Fleet gott out to them. They made in all about eighty Sail, divided into four Squadrons, commanded by his Lordſhip in Perſon, Sir *Francis Drake* Vice-Admiral, and the Rear-Admirals *Hawkins* and *Forbiſher.* But about one in the Afternoone, they came in Sighte of the *Spaniſh Armada* two Leagues to the Weſtward of the *Eddiſtone,* ſailing in the Form of a half Moon, the Points whereof were ſeven Leagues aſunder.

B

Before the Armada had even sailed into the Channel, the English had learned details of Spain's plans.

The word 'armada' was used to describe D-Day events during the Second World War, when the massive Allied invasion of occupied Europe took place across the English Channel in June 1944. It was a highly appropriate description of the Allied fleet.

At dawn on 6 June 1944 (D-Day), an armada of Allied ships set sail for the beaches of Normandy. This is a newspaper headline written after the event.

At sea with the invasion armada

The Royal Navy played a leading role in the great invasion and on these pages North-East D-day veterans tell their stories

I WAS serving in the Royal Navy during the war, operating on the Russian convoys on the cruiser HMS Belfast.

About the last week in May 1944 we were withdrawn from these operations and sailed from Scapa Flow into the Clyde.

We were there for a day or two and during this time we were joined by a number of other naval ships.

Just prior to midnight on June 4 we took to sea and turned south down the Irish Sea. I had the midnight to 4am watch and was stationed on the bridge for defence position.

About 3.30am we were near

6 I could see lots of ships of all sizes, cruisers, destroyers and landing craft coming out of every bay and cove . . . 9

My part in naval history

Under fire but we hit back

MY ship HMS Clematis was at anchor in Sheerness previous to sailing to Arromanch in Normandy to take part in the initial landings on June 6, 1944.

While in Sheerness all shore leave was stopped so we had a good idea what was going to happen.

Eventually the captain cleared lower deck and informed us that we were taking part in what turned out to be one of the largest invasions in history. I will never forget the scenes as we set sail, ships as far as we could see on the horizon and the sky filled with various types.

On arrival at Arromanch we were anchored next to the battleship Rodney and the cruiser Belfast who were bombarding the coastal fortifications. We were closed up at day and night at action stations and supplied with a small tin of action rations because it was impossible to go below deck for a meal.

MAPPING THE WORLD

I n the Middle Ages the Mediterranean Sea was the
centre of the known world. At the beginning of the
15th century, Portuguese sailing ships started to
explore the Atlantic. They moved southwards, hugging
the coast of West Africa, and eventually reached India.

A 16th-century map of the world.

*The first European to land in North
America was Sebastian Cabot. He reached
Newfoundland in 1497. Cabot later
opened up trade routes between England
and Russia. Merchant ships were to play an
important part in the defence of England
against the Spanish Armada. This seal die
belonged to a 16th-century merchant trader.*

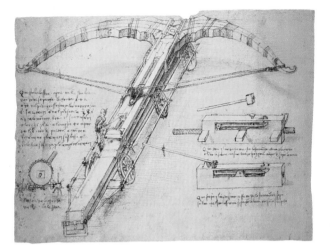

The Renaissance was a time when science and technology flourished. This giant catapult was designed by Leonardo da Vinci.

This newspaper headline refers to a 20th-century conflict between Spanish fishermen and Canadians in Newfoundland – 500 years after Cabot landed there.

Meanwhile the explorer Christopher Columbus had travelled westwards with his Spanish ships to discover the New World of the Americas. At that time it was believed that Asia lay across the Atlantic Ocean. By the 16th century, Spanish and Portuguese traders had reached the Far East. Both countries established vast empires – the Portuguese in the east and the Spanish in the west. A new class of wealthy merchants emerged. These men became patrons of the arts, encouraging the Renaissance or 'new learning' that was then sweeping through Europe.

Netted, suspects from the armada of greed

By SUZANNE O'SHEA

THEIR names sounded English. But there was one sure way of telling the trawlers Lady Laura and Skellig Light were really Spanish.

Yesterday, detained in the harbour of Killybegs, County Donegal, they were the only vessels not flying the Canadian flag. In the streets of this fishing village on the edge of the Atlantic, the Maple Leaf emblem could also be seen hanging from shops, as locals expressed their support for the Canadians in their battle with Spanish fishermen.

9

CATHOLIC SPAIN

Philip II of Spain

By the 1550s the Spanish had settled in their New World territories. They had destroyed the ancient civilisations of the Incas and the Aztecs and had plundered the rich silver mines. Laden with loot, Spanish treasure ships sailed from the New World to Spain. The Portuguese had settled in Brazil, where sugar plantations worked by slave labour were set up.

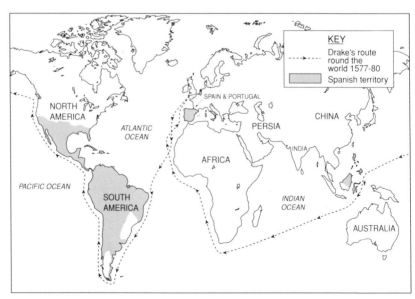

By 1580 Spain held the Low Countries (now known as Belgium, Luxembourg and the Netherlands), Mexico, Portugal and its empire, much of Italy, and the new lands of the Americas.

This amusing picture from 1580 shows the Low Countries as a cow being fed by Elizabeth I of England, ridden by Philip II of Spain and milked by William, Prince of Orange and Protestant leader of the Dutch. Spanish troops were to be ferried from the Low Countries to England during the Armada campaign.

Soon the infamous slave trade between West Africa and South America became another source of wealth for the Spanish and Portuguese. By 1580 Philip II of Spain, a devout Roman Catholic, had absorbed the Portuguese Empire into his own vast Spanish Empire. At that time he was the most powerful figure in Europe and his army, led by the Duke of Parma, the most feared. Philip wanted to crush all opposition to the Catholic Church.

In what became known as the St Bartholomew's Eve Massacre, 50,000 Protestants were killed in one day in Paris. The Catholic Philip II of Spain and the Protestant Elizabeth I of England were bitter enemies.

PIRATES

Francis Drake

The Protestant Queen Elizabeth I of England – enemy of the Catholic Philip II of Spain – did not always favour Francis Drake, the infamous seafarer and the first Englishman to sail round the world. Nevertheless she encouraged his looting raids on Spanish treasure ships and in 1585 she gave him a fleet to attack the Spanish Americas. Drake captured Cartagena in Colombia and St Augustine in Florida.

A page from the journal of Francis Fletcher, the chaplain on board the Golden Hinde *during Drake's voyage round the world*

In this picture of Drake's attack on Cartagena in 1586, English troops are seen marching on the town. At the bottom right is an iguana – a local reptile.

The Spanish bank collapsed temporarily because of Drake's plundering of Cartagena. The Spanish saw Drake as a villainous pirate but to the English he was the national hero who dared to challenge their enemy, Spain. Between 1577 and 1580 Drake had circumnavigated the world in his famous ship, the *Golden Hinde*.

The only remaining bars of gold from 16th-century Spanish treasure ships can be seen today in the British Museum in London.

13

SIR FRANCIS DRAKE

A s one of the greatest Elizabethan seamen, Drake was made second in command of the English fleet that lined up as the Spanish Armada approached the English coast. Born in Devon in south-west England, Drake was a short, red-haired man, full of self-confidence and ambition. He served the queen bravely, while at the same time making himself very rich.

Inside Buckland Abbey, Drake's home, there is the replica of a chair made from the oak timbers of the Golden Hinde.

Drake's drum was carried into battle all over the world. Legend has it that should England ever be in danger again, the drum will sound and summon Drake to the rescue.

14

Queen Elizabeth I knighted Drake on the Thames riverside in London. Drake's sword can be seen today on the ship HMS Drake *at Devonport, near Plymouth.*

Elizabeth knighted Drake after his circumnavigation of the world. She was delighted on his return to see the *Golden Hinde* laden with treasure. Drake was able to purchase Buckland Abbey in Devon with his share of the booty. In 1587 Drake's daring attack on Cadiz delayed Spain's preparations for the Armada campaign by a whole year. Drake died of fever in Panama in Central America and was buried at sea. Attempts may soon be made to retrieve his coffin.

This is a modern replica of the Golden Hinde – *the famous galleon that took Drake round the world.*

SLAVERY

Sir John Hawkins' son Richard commanded the Swallow *during the Armada campaign. He was later captured and held prisoner in South America for 12 years.*

Francis Drake's cousin, John Hawkins, was responsible for the design of the new English ships that were to prove superior to the huge Spanish galleons of the Armada. He was also the first Englishman to be associated with the rising trade in slaves. As a result Hawkins' name is less honoured today than it might have been. Between 1562 and 1569 Hawkins made three voyages to the West Indies and the coast of South America. He became rich from the slave trade, trading African slaves from the Guinea coast for gold, silver and pearls from the Caribbean.

Sir John Hawkins was the first English slave trader.

In the 16th century, slaves from West Africa were put to work in the gold and silver mines of the New World and on the sugar plantations.

Hawkins was the first Englishman to challenge Spain's domination of the Americas and pirates like Drake followed his example. Hawkins was knighted by Elizabeth I for his role before and during the attempted Spanish invasion.

This newspaper headline shows how people's attitudes have changed since Sir John Hawkins' time.

Slave trade returns to haunt architect of Armada victory

By Andrew Pierce

PLANS to celebrate the 400th anniversary of the death of Sir John Hawkins, knighted for his part in the victory over the Armada, have fallen victim to political correctness.

Plymouth City Council, which last year tried to ban th

when the conditions of mariners were greatly improved. As well as the knighthood for his pivotal role against the Armada, he was made a vice-admiral by a grateful monarch.

understated in naval history."

Dame Janet Fookes, (C, Plymouth Drake), said: "I thought I had heard it all when they tried to ban 'manager'. There was such

NAVIGATING

A lodestone is a piece of naturally magnetic rock that was used to remagnetise the needle of the ship's compass.

Many artefacts from Elizabethan times have survived and can be seen in museums. From examples of navigation tools and charts, it is possible to imagine the difficulties that must have faced seamen at that time. Early navigators needed landmarks to fix their position. This is why the first explorers clung to the coast-lines, afraid to travel into uncharted waters.

An astrolabe is a model of the heavens reproduced on a flat surface. Mariners in the 16th century used astrolabes to work out astronomical measurements.

This 16th-century mariner's compass has gimbal mountings to keep the bowl steady at sea.

Latitude could be calculated using an astrolabe to measure the height of the sun or the pole star, but working out longitude remained a problem until the invention of the ship's clock. The first printed sea atlas was published in 1584 by Waghenaer, a Dutch master pilot. It contained charts and directions for the coasts of Europe. In 1588 it was translated into English and published as *The Mariners' Mirrour*.

Francis Drake used a collection of navigational instruments like this astronomical compendium, which gave compass direction and latitude bearings.

NEW SHIPS

The permanent English navy began in Tudor times. By 1513 King Henry VIII had 30 ships to use against France. Portsmouth dockyard on the south coast of England had been founded in 1495. New dockyards were built at Woolwich, Deptford and Erith along the River Thames. Early Tudor ships were high-sided with 'castles' for close fighting. The new galleons designed by John Hawkins for Elizabeth I were faster. They also relied on guns firing a broadside from a distance to defeat the enemy. The navy that defended England against the Spanish Armada was the most powerful in Europe.

'castle'

This old-style ship has the high 'castle', which was useful for close fighting.

The Mary Rose, *one of Henry VIII's flagships, sank in Portsmouth harbour in 1545. It has recently been salvaged and historians are learning a great deal about Tudor ships from it.*

Of Elizabeth's 34 ships, 17 were modern galleons built in the 1570s and 1580s. These were known as race-built ships and were sleeker and better armed than any other ships of that size.

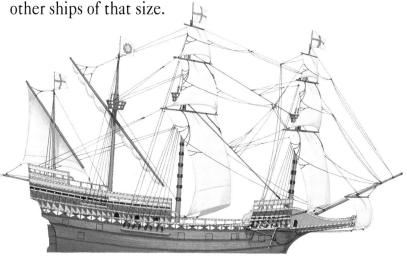

The new galleons were called 'race-built' ships because the 'castle' had been razed (removed) to make them sleeker and easier to manoeuvre.

PROTESTANT ENGLAND

The Protestant Elizabeth I of England succeeded her Catholic half-sister, Mary I, in 1558. Elizabeth did not marry and ruled alone for 45 years. She had such an impact on English life that those years are known as the Elizabethan age. For most of her reign the Catholic Philip II of Spain was her enemy, although he did once offer her marriage. Henry VIII, father of Mary and Elizabeth, had broken from the Catholic Church in order to divorce Mary's mother, the Spanish Catherine of Aragon.

Philip II of Spain was married to Mary I of England for four years until her death. They were both devout Catholics.

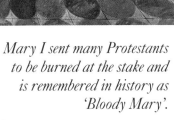

Mary I sent many Protestants to be burned at the stake and is remembered in history as 'Bloody Mary'.

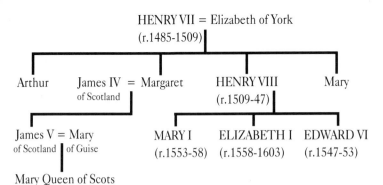

HENRY VII = Elizabeth of York
(r.1485-1509)

Arthur   James IV = Margaret   HENRY VIII   Mary
           of Scotland   (r.1509-47)

James V = Mary   MARY I   ELIZABETH I   EDWARD VI
of Scotland | of Guise (r.1553-58) (r.1558-1603) (r.1547-53)

Mary Queen of Scots

Mary Queen of Scots was a distant cousin of Elizabeth I. She spent her childhood in France.

Henry had then set up the Protestant Church of England with himself as the head of it. Mary Queen of Scots, who was Elizabeth's cousin and a Catholic, also claimed the English throne and was supported by Philip. Mary was kept under close guard by Elizabeth and was executed in 1587 after a Catholic plot was uncovered. This angered Philip.

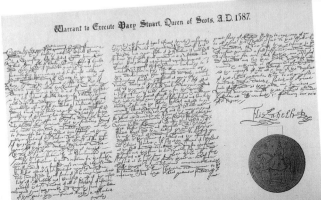

Elizabeth reluctantly signed this warrant ordering the execution of Mary Queen of Scots. The execution took place on 7 February 1587.

ELIZABETH I

The Elizabethan age was a period of great achievement in English history. The queen's coronation was a lavish occasion that lasted several days. Elizabeth rode through London in a golden palanquin, with a canopy of red velvet above her head.

In this famous painting of Queen Elizabeth I, known as the Armada Portrait, *scenes from the Armada campaign are shown in the background.*

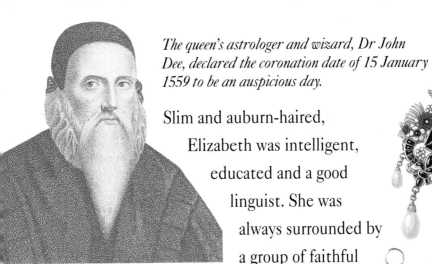

The queen's astrologer and wizard, Dr John Dee, declared the coronation date of 15 January 1559 to be an auspicious day.

Slim and auburn-haired, Elizabeth was intelligent, educated and a good linguist. She was always surrounded by a group of faithful admirers and followers but she never became friends with her Catholic half-sister, Mary I. Philip II of Spain denounced Elizabeth as a heretic. Already angry at Francis Drake's acts of piracy against Spanish treasure ships, Philip was incensed when Elizabeth knighted Drake. The execution of Mary Queen of Scots further angered him. The final straw was when Drake attacked Cadiz in 1587 and so 'singed the King of Spain's beard'.

In the 16th century the borderline between science and magic was unclear. People still believed in witches.

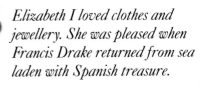

Elizabeth I loved clothes and jewellery. She was pleased when Francis Drake returned from sea laden with Spanish treasure.

ADMIRALS AND SPIES

The English fleet was commanded by Charles Howard of Effingham, Lord High Admiral, even though he had little naval experience. Sir Francis Drake was Vice Admiral of the Fleet and his flagship was called *Revenge*. Sir John Hawkins in his flagship, *Victory*, was Rear Admiral. Lord Henry Seymour was Admiral of the Narrow Seas. His ships guarded the Straits of Dover and the River Thames.

Howard's flagship was the Ark Royal. *It had once been called the* Ark Raleigh, *because Sir Walter Raleigh had given it to the queen when he owed her £5000.*

Charles Howard

Sir Walter Raleigh was made Captain of the Queen's Guard in 1587. He was responsible for Elizabeth's safety. During the attempted Spanish invasion, he organised the defence of Devon and Cornwall.

Elizabeth I called Secretary of State Sir Francis Walsingham her 'spy'. He created a spy network to protect her against foreign enemies. He was one of the most powerful men at court.

During Elizabeth I's reign the religious conflict led to a number of Catholic plots against her. It was at this time that the first English secret service began, headed by Sir Francis Walsingham. In 1586 he uncovered the Catholic plot that was to lead to the execution of Mary Queen of Scots. He was aware of Philip II's Armada plans so England was well prepared.

Walsingham's agents discovered Philip II's invasion plans when the plans were printed for everyone to read even before the Armada left Lisbon.

SINGEING THE KING OF SPAIN'S BEARD

Elizabeth did her best to avoid all-out war with Spain, but Philip was determined that his Armada should set sail. In April 1587 Elizabeth's 'pirate', Francis Drake, further infuriated Philip when he made a surprise attack on Spanish ships anchored in Cadiz harbour. Chaos broke out as Drake plundered ruthlessly, sinking or capturing 37 Spanish ships.

Drake's raid on Spanish ships in Cadiz harbour in 1587 was said to have 'singed the King of Spain's beard'. This attack delayed the sailing of the Spanish Armada.

Four galleasses from Naples were part of the Spanish Armada.
A galleass had sails and oars.

The immediate effect was that Philip had to postpone
the Armada for a year. But there was also a very
important side-effect of Drake's raid – barrel staves
made from seasoned wood had been destroyed. This
meant that 'green' wood was used to make the barrels
in which food and water for the Armada were stored.
As the wood dried the barrels shrank and split and the
contents were ruined.

BEACONS BLAZE

An attempt was made to inflict damage on the Spanish Armada before it reached England but the weather forced the English fleet to turn back. On 22 July the English fleet dropped anchor in Plymouth Sound to wait for the Spanish. Beacons stood at strategic points across England, ready to be lit as soon as the enemy was sighted. There were watchers at each beacon, who were paid eight pence (8d) a day.

John Norris, nicknamed 'Black Jack', was a commander of the English troops.

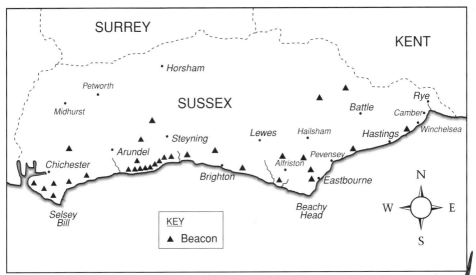

The beacon system was vital to England's coastal defence.

Watchers had the wood from three trees to fuel the blaze. A hut was provided, but without seats in case the watchers fell asleep. Militiamen and volunteers were mustered to defend the southern shores of England. Additional armies had to be raised in and around London and further north. This was necessary because the total population of Elizabethan England was only about 3.5 million.

By June 1588 there were 27,000 foot soldiers and 2,500 soldiers on horseback ready to fight the Spanish.

SHIPS IN SIGHT

The Spanish commander Santa Cruz, who organised the Armada, died before it sailed. The command was given to the less experienced Duke of Medina Sidonia, who suffered from seasickness. In May 1588 he led the Armada out of Lisbon harbour in Portugal. The intention was to rendezvous off the coast of the Spanish Netherlands with troops led by the Duke of Parma. This invasion force would then be ferried in barges across the Channel to occupy England. The weather was poor and it took the Armada 13 days to reach northern Spain.

The Duke of Parma commanded the Spanish army in the Netherlands. He was the greatest general of the age. According to Philip II's plan, Parma was to land an army of invasion in England with the Armada acting mainly as transport for troops and equipment. Parma thought the plan was unworkable.

When the Armada was first sighted by the English fleet in Plymouth Sound on 30 July, Drake was there in his ship Revenge.

News of the Spanish Armada's approach was brought to Francis Drake by Captain Thomas Fleming. Drake had time to finish his game of bowls because he knew the tides along the south-west coast of England.

Food and water had gone bad, so the Spanish fleet headed ashore. Repairs were carried out and fresh supplies were taken on board. Then storms sank five ships. The Armada finally reformed and on 29 July the Lizard Point in Cornwall was sighted.

This cartoon from Punch *magazine shows Winston Churchill also playing bowls as German invaders threaten England during the Second World War.*

INTO BATTLE

The less well-armed ships of the Armada were in the centre of the crescent shape, protected by the two 'horns' that formed a fighting escort.

The Armada formed a crescent shape seven miles wide as it began its slow journey up the Channel. The English fleet had left Plymouth to anchor at Rame Head further out in the Channel. It was important for sailing ships in battle to have the wind, or 'weather gage', behind them. On 31 July Howard had the weather gage. The first action was off Plymouth. On 3 August there was minor action off the Isle of Wight.

This 'morion' helmet was worn by a Spanish officer.

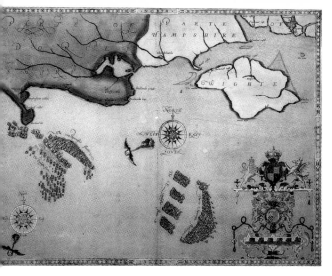

In August 1588 the Spanish Armada met the English fleet in a battle off Portland Bill. Sir Martin Frobisher in his ship Triumph *was caught against the shore but the tides prevented the Spanish from reaching him. Then the wind changed direction and Frobisher escaped.*

Howard then organised four independent squadrons. He commanded one and the other commands were given to Drake, Hawkins and Sir Martin Frobisher. The nimble English ships could manoeuvre to fire broadsides, while the Spanish looked desperately for opportunities to board. These running skirmishes ended when the Spanish anchored off Calais on the French coast on 7 August.

The Spanish ship Rosario *was damaged in a collision and the* San Salvador *was gutted by an accidental explosion on board that killed 200 men. These ships were taken by the English. Drake took the* Rosario.

FIRESHIPS ADRIFT

message was sent to Parma telling him that the
Armada had reached Calais. But he did not receive
it until 8 August. By the time Parma and his troops
arrived on 9 August the Armada had already been
driven into the North Sea by gales. Aware that the
intended rendezvous had to be prevented, the English
had attacked the Armada with fireships at midnight on
7 August. Medina Sidonia had ordered his ships to slip
their cables and return to collect their anchors when
the fireships had burnt out.

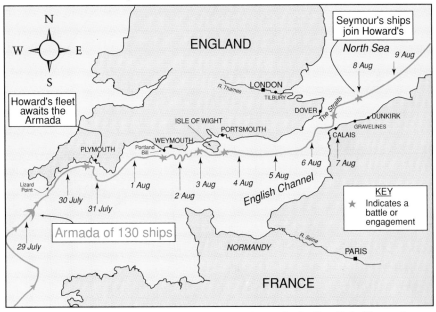

The pursuit of the Spanish Armada through the English Channel.

Fire was one of the greatest hazards facing 16th-century timber ships. Small, unmanned boats filled with highly inflammable materials could be set alight and cast adrift where the wind would carry them into enemy ships at anchor. This painting is an imaginary version of English fireships attacking the Spanish Armada, as the whole incident took place in darkness.

But by the morning the tide had drawn the Spanish fleet too far to return. The disciplined formation of the Armada had also been broken. So the English had challenged individual ships and in the ensuing Battle of Gravelines the Spanish had suffered heavy losses.

These 17th-century playing cards feature the Spanish Armada. Catholic priests are shown as knaves.

BAD WEATHER

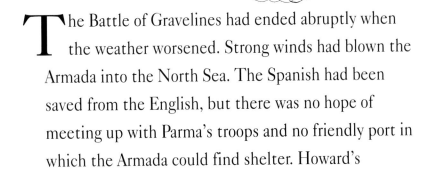

T he Battle of Gravelines had ended abruptly when the weather worsened. Strong winds had blown the Armada into the North Sea. The Spanish had been saved from the English, but there was no hope of meeting up with Parma's troops and no friendly port in which the Armada could find shelter. Howard's squadron pursued the remnants of the Spanish fleet as far as the Firth of Forth in southern Scotland and then turned back. On 19 August Elizabeth I addressed her troops at Tilbury on the River Thames.

The English commanders decided to pursue the Armada as it tried to escape. They signed this resolution after a council of war.

The Armada carried a number of horses and mules on board. When the Spanish ships were swept northwards, the animals were thrown into the sea because of the shortage of drinking water.

The Armada continued its hazardous journey back to Spain, via the far northern tip of Scotland. One-third of the Armada was either lost at sea or wrecked on the coast of Scotland or Ireland. Two-thirds of the 30,000 men who sailed from Lisbon never returned.

Elizabeth I wore an armoured breastplate like this one when she spoke to her troops at Tilbury in August 1588.

SHIPWRECKED

On 21 August the broken Armada altered its course for Spain and sailed into the Atlantic Ocean. The fierce storms that it encountered there were to scatter the fleet completely. The exhausted crews had little food left and most of what remained was rotten. Although it was summer the weather was freezing and the men had no warm clothing. As they manned the pumps in those stormy seas they must have suffered utter despair. By September the remaining ships were fighting desperately to avoid shipwreck on the rocky coast of Ireland as they struggled against Atlantic gales.

The Armada did not have accurate navigation charts of the Irish coast so many ships were wrecked on Achill Head.

More than 24 ships were lost off the Irish coast. On 23 September Sidonia's flagship, *San Martin*, finally arrived in northern Spain, four months after setting sail.

From SCOTLAND

LACADA POINT
LONDONDERRY
ACHILL HEAD
IRELAND
DUBLIN
GALWAY
LIMEI
CORK

To SPAIN

KEY
★ Shipwreck

The Spanish sailed north around the Scottish coast, then west and south down the western coast of Ireland.

The English did not lose any ships during the Armada campaign.

ESTIMATE OF SPANISH SHIPS LOST	
Galleons	4
Warships	18
Hulks	11
Small craft	15
Galleasses	2
Galley	1
TOTAL	51

SALVAGED

T he last ship of
the Armada to be wrecked on the Irish coast was the
Girona. It sank on 26 October off Lacada Point in
County Antrim, Northern Ireland. There were 1,300
men on board – only five survived to be sheltered
by the McDonnell family at Dunluce Castle.
Many of the Spanish sailors who survived
shipwreck and struggled ashore were slaughtered
or held to ransom by the Irish.

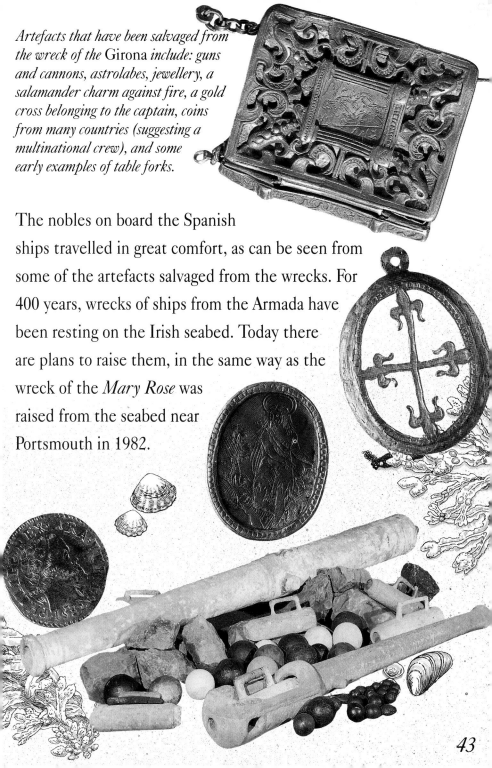

Artefacts that have been salvaged from the wreck of the Girona *include: guns and cannons, astrolabes, jewellery, a salamander charm against fire, a gold cross belonging to the captain, coins from many countries (suggesting a multinational crew), and some early examples of table forks.*

The nobles on board the Spanish ships travelled in great comfort, as can be seen from some of the artefacts salvaged from the wrecks. For 400 years, wrecks of ships from the Armada have been resting on the Irish seabed. Today there are plans to raise them, in the same way as the wreck of the *Mary Rose* was raised from the seabed near Portsmouth in 1982.

NAVAL POWER

Medal commemorating the defeat of the Spanish Armada.

After the Armada campaign, shipbuilding progressed rapidly in England. By the time of King Charles I, the first three-decker ship had been built. A lesson had been learned in 1588 and from then on the English navy was always in a state of readiness. Service medals were struck for the first time in 1588.

*He made the wynds and waters rise
To scatter all myne enemyes
This Josephes Lord and Israells god
The fyry piller and dayes clowde
That saved his saincts from wicked men
And drenshet the honor of the prowde
And hathe preservud in tender love
The spirit of his Turtle dove.*

This poem was written by Elizabeth I after the Armada campaign.

There have been many ships in the British navy called Ark Royal *since Howard's flagship. The latest one (page 45) was completed in 1986.*

In this famous 17th-century painting, the Spanish Armada is made to look like the dragon that St George, the patron saint of England, is said to have killed.

For many English Protestants the defeat of the Catholic Spanish Armada was seen as a sign that God was on their side. Commemorative medals were made with the inscription 'God blew and they were scattered'. But the Armada campaign was less a religious war than a war against a tyrant who was threatening invasion.

Ark Royal

The Armada Jewel is a miniature of Elizabeth I, surrounded by enamelled gold set with diamonds and rubies. It was made in about 1600.

GLOSSARY

beacon *A signal fire on a hill or tower, once used to warn of invasion.*

broadside *The firing of all the guns on one side of a warship.*

Cabot, Sebastian (1474-1557)
Italian-born explorer whose voyages on behalf of the English led to the growth of English colonies in North America.

Catholic *Someone who belongs to the Christian Roman Catholic Church.*

Drake, Sir Francis (1540-96)
A famous English seaman and pirate and the first man to sail around the world (1577-80). Drake played an important part in defeating the Spanish Armada.

galleass *A three-masted galley; a sailing ship that could also be rowed.*

galleon *A large sailing ship with three or more masts.*

galley *A boat powered only by oarsmen, often slaves. Galleys were used in the Mediterranean Sea by the Spanish and were still in use in 1588.*

gimbals *Pivotted rings making a device in which a compass can be suspended freely.*

Golden Hinde *The ship in which Drake sailed around the world. The hind is a deer.*

Gregorian calendar *The New Style (NS) calendar first introduced in Italy in 1582. England's failure to follow suit meant that it was 11 days behind the rest of Europe until 1752.*

Julian calendar *The Old Style (OS) calendar introduced by Julius Caesar.*

Leonardo da Vinci (1452-1519)
Italian artist, inventor, scientist and a genius of the Renaissance.

Low Countries *The part of Europe that now consists of Belgium, Luxembourg and the Netherlands.*

militia *A group of citizens enlisted for military service in times of emergency.*

Protestant *A Christian belonging to the Protestant Church of England, which was set up by Henry VIII when he broke away from the Catholic Church.*

Raleigh, Sir Walter (1552-1618)
Elizabethan adventurer who introduced potatoes and tobacco from the New World into England.

Spanish Netherlands *The countries that are now known as Belgium and the Netherlands.*

INDEX